AF324245

Guiding Light

THE TRUE WAY TO EMPOWERMENT

PRINCE HALL

Copyright © 2024 **Hall-Go Publishing LLC**

All rights reserved. No part of this publication may be reproduced, distributed, or transmitted in any form or by any means, including photocopying, recording, or other electronic or mechanical methods, without the prior written permission of the publisher, except in the case of brief quotations embodied in critical reviews and certain other noncommercial uses permitted by copyright law. For permission requests, write to the publisher, addressed "Attention: Book Rights and Permission," at the address below.

Published in the United States of America

ISBN 978-1-963379-35-8 (SC)
ISBN 978-1-963379-33-4 (HC)
ISBN 978-1-963379-34-1 (Ebook)

Hall-Go Publishing LLC
222 West 6th Street
Suite 400, San Pedro, CA, 90731
mikenice711@gmail.com

Order Information a
and Rights Permission:

Quantity sales. Special discounts might be available on quantity purchases by corporations, associations, and others. For details, contact the publisher at the address above.

For Book Rights Adaptation and other Rights Permission. Call us at toll-free 1-888-945-8513 or send us an email at admin@stellarliterary.com.

Contents

A story..8

Chapter 1 Mindset...11

Chapter 2 Your Health is your wealth 18

Chapter 3 Hold on by letting go 25

Chapter 4 Hygiene, Appearance, and Dress-code.............28

Chapter 5 Goals 33

Chapter 6 Butterfly effect 39

Note to the Reader 42

Chapter 7 Unleash your full potential...............................44

Chapter 8 Protect your crown...48

Chapter 9 Dig deeper..56

Chapter 10 Awaken your vocabulary 60

Chapter 11 Relationships, Friends or Foe 64

Chapter 12 Finances/Investing/Credit/Retirement 70

Chapter 13 Life insurance, will, and Funeral related matters. ...85

Poem...95

DEDICATION

This book is dedicated to my dear parents, Nerie and Mamie Hall, whose love and support have been my guiding light. Though my parents are no longer with us, I take comfort in knowing that they would have been proud to see this book completed. Their wisdom and encouragement continues to inspire me, and I am grateful for the lasting impact they have had on my life.

ACKNOWLEDGEMENTS

I would like to express my heartfelt gratitude to Mary Stanworth, my agent from Stellar Literary, my family and friends who believe in me and offered unwavering encouragement throughout this journey. Your support has been invaluable.

INTRODUCTION

Guiding light, began as a personal project intended to provide my children with a roadmap for navigating life's myriad journeys and challenges. As I delved deeper into its creation, I came to realize that its message could resonate with a wider audience. So with great enthusiasm, I extend a warm welcome to the Guiding Light, (The true way to empowerment)

The primary aim of this book is to inspire, motivate, inform and propel you into taking action. The chapters in this book are thoughtfully crafted to provide comprehensive and easily accessible content for individuals seeking to build a solid foundation for themselves.

A STORY

The Guardians of emotions, Powerful and Greatness, decided to host a grand celebration for all the emotions at the majestic castle of sentiments. Joy and Happiness arrived, their faces beaming with smiles. Love appeared, accompanied by a date who exuded flawless beauty. Numerous other emotions filled the castle and everyone was reveling in the festivities.

However, the atmosphere took a sudden turn when Envy and Hatred showed up at the castle. They began causing trouble, particularly targeting Greatness at the entrance.

Greatness, aware of the longstanding enmity between Love and Hatred, understood that granting entry to Hatred would be a disastrous idea. With a display of authority, Powerful approached the door and firmly requested that Hatred and his accomplice depart. Hatred, feeling greatly vexed but deterred by Powerful's immense strength, begrudgingly left the premises.

Little did anyone know that Envy had planted a seed of deviousness in Hatred's mind. They conspired to unleash chaos upon the castle, setting it ablaze.

The merriment inside muzzled the sound of their treacherous act, as flames engulfed the surroundings. Love, with his keen senes, caught a whiff of the burning scent and swiftly alerted everyone. Frantically, Love led the evacuation, ensuring the safety of all except himself. He found himself trapped, a sense of hopelessness creeping over.

In the depths of this dire situation, Time materialized before the ALMIGHTY in the heavens. Urgently informing him of Love's predicament. Without hesitation, GOD and Time appeared at the castle in an instant. With a snap of his divine fingers, GOD extinguished the raging fire.

Time, filled with gratitude, expressed his thanks to the ALMIGHTY. GOD instructed Time to find Love, assuring him that everything would be taken care of. As swiftly as Time appeared, he vanished on his mission to rescue love. Time approached Love, and they embrace wholeheartedly as they departed the castle of sentiments

The essence of this tale lies in the invaluable nature of Love and only Time knows how precious Love is.

In addition, if you take the Time to Love yourself, the ALMIGHTY will enter your castle and perform miracles. (SMILE)

CHAPTER 1
MINDSET

Life can indeed be filled with cruel and challenging moments, where hardships and difficulties seem to be constant companions. Such experiences may include the loss of loved ones, facing unfortunate circumstances, or going through a painful separation. However, I'm here to assure you that things can change, and there is hope on the horizon.

I understand firsthand how life's struggles can weigh heavily on our minds, causing us to feel depressed, stressed and overwhelmed. In my own journey, I learned that these difficulties are a natural part of life, and it is up to us to find the mental strength to navigate through them. I discovered power of meditation, self-reflection and seeking wisdom through reading. These practices opened a new world for me. Something profound and captivating.

The key to shifting your mental state lies in the ability to focus on the positives admidst the negatives. Instead of dwelling on what went wrong, I started seeking out the siver linings in every situation. For example, when running late, I shifted my thoughts to the possibility that I may have avoided an accident by being delayed. I began embracing the idea of seeing the cup half full rather than half empty. This positive way of thinking strengthened my mind and made me mentally stronger.

With this newfound mental resilience, I discovered a tunnel leading me to the next level of personal growth. My confidence soared, as i realized that i was capable of achieving whatever I set my mind to. I opened the door to my metaphorical castle and allowed the power of GOD- or whatever higher power you believe in- to work wonders in my life.

It was in that transformative moment that I truly began to love myself for the first time.

Meet Joe- your typical working guy, navigating the ebb and flow of everyday life. Joe's journey began when a dear friend introduced him to a series of mental strengthening programs, igniting within him a transformation that transcended the ordinary. These programs weren't just a source of inspiration; they became the catalyst for Joe's profound self-discovery and empowerment.

 One of the fundamental lessons that resonated deeply with Joe was the simple yet profound directive to "believe in yourself." It was a revelation that shattered the barriers of self-doubt and uncertainty that had long held him in their grip. In the past, Joe found himself plagued by incessant second- guessing, a relentless companion borne of a lack of confidence. But today, should you encounter Joe, you'd be stuck by the radiant aura of confidence that envelops him-a transformation so profound that one might be led to believe he himself conjured the sun, moon and stars into existence. Even the way he carries himself, the assuredness in his step, speaks volumes.

This, you see, is the undeniable power of the subconscious mind in harmony with the higher being. Joe's unwavering belief in his own capabilities is a testament to the profound connection he has forged with the force that renders all things possible. It's no longer a mere conviction; it's a deep-rooted knowledge that propels him to embrace life's challenges with unwavering resolve, knowing that he is truly capable of all things, for he is aligned with the higher being that orchestrates the very fabric of existence itself.

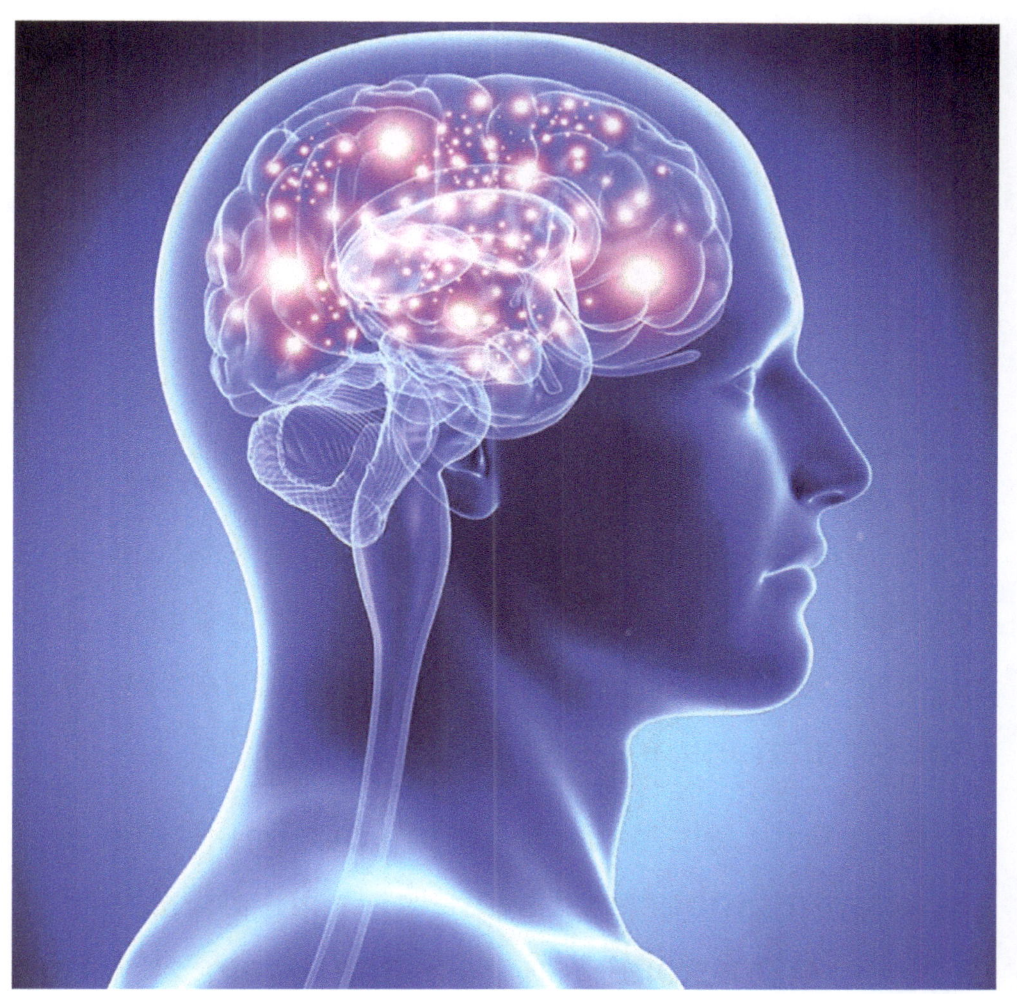

A transformative Mindset

Its incredible to witness how even overachievers, like celebrities, have found this information and utilized it to make positive changes in their lives. By embracing a mental shift and tapping into the well spring of self-love, they have accomplished great things. Now, the question I pose to you is: Do you love yourself enough to become one with the HIGHER POWER within you and unlock your potential, leading to greater achievements?

Let's embark on this journey of making that powerful mental shift together. Believe in the possibility of great things, for through self-love and aligning with your inner higher power, remarkable transformations are waiting to emerge.

Trust in yourself, have faith in your resilience and always remember that with the right mindset, all things are possible. You have the strength within you to overcome any challenge and create a life filled with joy, fulfillment and purpose.

So let's see what you're made of!!!!!! Embrace the mental shift, tap in the well of self-love, and let your life become a testament to the wonders that can be achieved when we believe in ourselves and the higher power that resides within each of us.

CHAPTER 2
YOUR HEALTH IS YOUR WEALTH

The saying, "your health is your wealth" emphasizes the importance of prioritizing one's well being, and diet plays a crucial role in maintaining good health. Our bodies are unique and irreplaceable, and its our responsibility to take care of them through proper nutrition and balance diet.

When it comes to dieting, it is important to adopt a sustainable and balance approach. Extreme eating patterns may yield short –term results, but they can be detrimental to long term health. Instead, focusing on a well rounded diet that includes a variety of whole foods. Such as fruits, vegetables, whole grains, lean proteins is the key.

A healthy diet positively impacts energy levels and sleep quality . Nutrient- dense foods provides energy throughout the day, while excessive consumption of process foods high in sugar and unhealthy fats may lead to fatique.

It is worth noting that everyone's dietary needs may vary depending on factors such as age, sex, activity level, and underlying health conditions. Consulting with a healthcare professional or registered dietitian can provide personalized guidance and support in creating a diet plan that suits your needs.

EXERCISE

Exercise is a crucial component of self – improvement and maintaining good health. By setting aside three days each week for a rounded exercise program, you can significantly enhance your overall being. A diverse range of physical activities such as walking, jogging, running on the treadmill, weight lifting and calisthenics can help you achieve holistic fitness. By establishing a strong mind –body connection through exercise. You can pave the way for a healthier and more fulfilling life. The benefits of regular exercise extend beyond physical fitness. Positively, it impacts mental and emotional well being as well.

Meet: Mikenzie and Mikayla

Two inseparable best friends who have shared a bond since their early school days. Despite their enduring friendship, they have approached life's challenges in contrasting ways. Mikenzie, with her unwavering determination, adopted a positive mindset when faced with adversity. She proactively tactled her problems and prioritized her well being by incorporating a structured workout plan into her lifestyle.

Mikenzie's commitment to staying physically active not only helped her manage stress effectively but also served as a source of resilience during difficult times. Her dedication to nurturing a healthy body and mind has been a guiding light, empowering her to confront obstacles with a newfound strength and vigor.

Conversely, Mikayla grappled with her tribulations in a markedly different manner. When besieged by stress, she sought solace in unhealthy eating habits and neglected to prioritize her well being. Consequently, she now finds herself contending with a myriad of health issues, the repercussions of neglecting her physical and mental health.

Had Mikayla embraced Mikenzie's positive ideology and commitment to regular exercise, she might have found herself in a far healthier position today. By incorporating Mikenzie's approach of valuing physical activity as a means to alleviate stress and maintaining a resilient mindset, Mikayla could have potentially averted the health issues that now disrupt her daily life.

As a result of her declining health, Mikayla frequently finds herself absent from work, continually attempting to play catch-up. This perpetual cycle not only affects her professional life but also takes a toll on her overall well being.

In learning from Mikenzie's example, Mikayla is beginning to realize the profound impact of prioritizing her health and well being. As she takes the steps to incorporate positive lifestyle changes, including dieting, regular exercise and a resilient mindset, she is gradually steering her life towards a path of improved health and vitality. Through

Mikenzie's unwavering support and guidance, Mikayla is now on a journey of self-discovery.

Therefore, its important to carve out time in your schedule for proper dieting and exercise, as the rewards will be well worth the effort. Your future self will undoubtedly express gratitude for the positive impact that dieting and exercise brings to your life, and always remember this one thing,

"Your health is your wealth"

CHAPTER 3
HOLD ON BY LETTING GO

Many of us unwittingly sacrifice our own happiness and sanity by clinging onto grudges and harboring meaningless emotions that we store away deep within ourselves. To truly empower ourselves, we must learn the art of letting go. It is through this act of release that we paradoxically hold onto our power. I am a firm believer in the transformative power of practicing forgiveness. By cleansing our spirits of all negatives that weigh us down, we can release the mental demons that haunt us and walk proudly and freely.

There exists an old saying among angels that to earn your wings, one must undergo a three way cleansing process of the mind, body and soul. I find this concept deeply intriguing and relevant to our human experience. It underscores the importance of tending to our holistic well-being and the interconnectedness of our inner and outer selves.

It is of paramount importance to unburden ourselves from the weight of the world that we carry on our shoulders. Let us embark on new journeys. By doing so, we liberate ourselves from the shackles of the past and open ourselves to the boundless possibilities of the present and the future.

Holding on by letting go is akin to a process of shedding the old to make way for the new. Its similar to emptying an old glass of water that has sat overnight, allowing us to refill it with a more pure and refreshing alternative. In this sense, we hold onto the positives, release the negatives, and create space for more positivity to flow into our lives.

In this act of renewal, we affirm our commitment to holding onto the virtues, aspirations, and values that align with our higher selves. Through this intentional letting go, we make room for the infusion of fresh perspectives, new opportunities, and a more authentic expression of who we are becoming.

In essence, holding on by letting go is an ongoing process of self –empowerment and self-renewal. It is a conscious choice to shed the layers of the past, creating an open space for emergence of our best selves.

CHAPTER 4
HYGIENE, APPEARANCE, AND DRESS-CODE

I couldn't stress it enough the importance of a good appearance, adhering to a nice dress- code, and practicing good hygiene. Some individuals may not care how they present themselves to the world, but it's crucial to at least uphold a good appearance for one's own sake, what I've noticed is that it can significantly boost your confidence. Furthermore, your appearance can influence the way people interact with you.

The era of smelling like oysters and animal poop is long gone, and rightfully so. It's absolutely repulsive!! It's a high time for a significant transformation. And by that, I don't mean changing the coins in your pocket.

Often, we fail to recognize the various agents that our bodies come into contact with, such as germs, bacteria, and negative energy that lingers in the environment. When these substances interact with our skin, our sweat glands kick into action, producing sweat that traps these agents in our body hair and gives rise to unpleasant odors.

Believe me,,, I could expound deeper into this topic for hours on end. So I'll move on. But know this, its time to embrace a change. let's make it happen!!!! SHOWER once or twice a day!!!

In my case, as the owner of a small delivery service, I've interacted with thousands of people over the years, which has honed my people skills and observational acumen. One particular day stands out, as it made me realize how a small shift in attire can alter the way people treat you.

As I was unloading boxes of beauty supplies from my truck, the owner of the goods made eye contact and recognized his merchandise. Despite this, when he got out of his vehicle, both of us approaching the store entrance, he let the door slam shut, almost in my face. I brushed it off, helped him with his delivery, and went about my business.

However, later on that day, upon returning home, I noticed that the blade of my hair clippers was dull. After a quick shower, I dressed in well pressed suit, polished shoes and adorned a tie. I decided to revisit the beauty supply store.

I have to admit, I was completely unrecognizable, and the timing couldn't have been more perfect. As I approached the beauty supply store, the owner was making his exit. However, he stopped in his tracks and held the door open for me. Seizing the opportunity, I leisurely dragged my feet and even took a moment to brush off my sparkling shoe. I exchanged his kind gesture with a warm thank you as I entered the store. While browsing and picking up a few items, I couldn't help but notice that the owner hadn't left; he was still lingering in the store.

When I went to cash out, I casually inquired of the cashier, "Does the owner have a twin brother?" Without giving her a chance to respond, I continued, knowing that the owner was within earshot. I recounted the morning delivery and how the individual had let the door slam on me while I was laden with supplies. Then, I mentioned how, on this occasion, what seemed to be the same person had gone out of his way to be helpful when I was empty – handed. I expressed my confusion and asked again, leaving room for her to interject. She confirmed that he didn't have any brothers. To cut a long story short, the next time I made a delivery to the store, the owner was exceedingly helpful, and he had gained himself a loyal customer.

In conclusion, people certainly respond to you differently when you take the time to clean up and present yourself well.

CHAPTER 5
GOALS

Setting goals can have a transformative effect on your life, shaping it in significant ways. Without clear objectives, you may find yourself drifting aimlessly, like a leaf being carried away by whims of the wind. However, when you establish meaningful goals, you attain a sense of direction and purpose.

IDLE TIME IS THE DEVIL'S PLAYGROUND

MEET: Mi'king

Idle time often leans to trouble, and with an abundance of free time and no clear goals, Mi'king found himself associating with the wrong crowd. These so-called friends continuously pressured him to partake in their drug addictions and bad habits. If Mi'king had established a solid set of goals, a regular routine, or a better way of directing his energy, he likely would have resisted the influence of these false friends and avoided the destructive path that lay ahead. Sometimes, having well – defined goals can keep you occupied and focused, steering clear of negative influences.

The act of setting goals also encourages personal growth and development. When you set ambitious yet attainable objectives, you challenge yourself to expand your skills, knowledge and capabilities. As you strive towards these goals, you inevitably encounter obstacles and setbacks. However, it is through overcoming these hurdles, you cultivate perseverance and adaptability. Each step becomes a learning opportunity, fostering your personal growth. Moreover, when you have a clear vision of what you want to accomplish, you are more likely to stay motivated and driven, even when faced with difficulties.

Goals serve as a reminder of your purpose, fueling your determination to push through any setbacks. So embrace the power of goal setting and unlock your full potential.

So we're going to talk about how you can turn your dreams into reality by setting clear short-term and long-term goals. I believe that writing down your goals and looking at them regularly is crucial, and I'm here to guide you through the process.

LONG-TERM GOAL:

Imagine this; you want to save $20,000 in the next few years. It's a big, audacious goal, but it's definitely achievable with the right plan in place.

SHORT-TERM GOAL:

Now, let's break it down. Your short-term goal might be to save $100 every week without touching it. Over a 4-year period, you would have saved a little over $20,000. It's amazing how those small, consistent steps add up to something significant, isn't it?

IMPORTANCE OF WRITING DOWN GOALS:

I can't stress this enough: writing down your goals makes them real. It's not just a thought in your head; it's a tangible commitment to yourself. So, grab a pen and paper and jot down those goals. Trust me, it makes a world of difference.

REINFORCING GOAL VISIBILITY:

You want these goals to be at the forefront of your mind, so put them in places where you'll see them every day. Stick them on your bathroom mirror, set digital reminders on your phone, or carry a small note with your goals written on it. The more you see them, the more you'll stay focused.

COMMITMENT TO PERSONAL GROWTH:

Taking goal setting seriously is a commitment to your own growth and happiness. It's your life, and setting meaningful goals is a powerful way to steer it in the direction you want.

By the way, if you don't have any goals, I highly recommend that you get some!!!

CHAPTER 6
BUTTERFLY EFFECT

They say when a butterFLY flaps its wings in New York, it can cause earthquakes in California. It's a powerful reminder that even the smallest actions can have far-reaching consequences.

Nevertheless, aren't you tired of crawling on your knees, stuck in the dirt like a caterpillar? It's time to transform, to earn your wings and take flight. You can't just sit there, looking sick and pathetic, doing nothing with your life. It's time to break free from the everyday routines that lead to nowhere. It's time to cause earthquakes, to make your presence known. You're not a nobody-you were born with a purpose, and you're here for a reason!!!

It's time to delve into the depths of existence, to step away from everyone and everything, and emerge twice as strong, sharper than a razor, more focused than ever. It's time to take flight, guiding by your inner light. Brush off your wings and believe in yourself-you got this!!!!! This transformation is about you, and it's time to embrace it with all your might.

The butterfly effect isn't just about chaos theory-it's about your potential to create waves of change. So, spread your wings and let your spirit soar. Embrace the unknown, unleash your strength, and make your mark on the world. The time for transformation is now.

You've been given the gift of life, with a unique blend of talents, experiences, and perspectives that only you possess. Embrace this uniqueness and let it fuel your journey of transformation. See yourself as a canvas waiting to be painted with the vibrant colors of your dreams and aspiration. You have the power to shape your reality and leave your mark on the world.

Above all, remember that the power to effect change lies within you. You hold the key to your own metamorphosis, and your potential is limitless. Embrace the transformative journey with open arms, for it will shape you into the person you are destined to become.

I see your wings growing already, you got this!!!!

NOTE TO THE READER

Dear Reader,

Congratulations on reaching to this point in the book. Your commitment to exploring the Guiding Light within these pages is truly commendable. As you continue on this journey, I want to express my utmost pride in your dedication to self improvement. Your willingness to engage with material like this speaks volumes about your determination to grow and evolve.

I assure you that the best is yet to come. Stay tuned for what lies ahead, as the upcoming chapters are sure to enrich your understanding and inspire further reflection. I sincerely hope that the insights shared will resonate with you, guiding you toward new perspectives and opportunities for personal development.

I believe that you will benefit greatly from the remaining content, and I encourage you to embrace the wisdom it offers. Remember, the journey toward self improvement is a remarkable path, and your commitment to it is an achievement in itself.

Thank you for embarking on this transformative journey with me. Enjoy the discoveries that await you within these pages.

With warm regards,

Mike Hall

CHAPTER 7
UNLEASH YOUR FULL POTENTIAL

MEET: Mikel

Mikel was undeniably gifted academically with an IQ of 150, and effortlessly excelled in his classes throughout his school years. However, his natural intelligence sometimes made him feel out of place and even a little ashamed as he struggled to find his place in the world. As he transitioned into adulthood, Mikel found opting for the path of least resistance, content with implementing easy revenue strategies. His approach which he dubbed "gas them up", involved presenting himself well dressed and parking his car at a local supermarket. There, he would grab his gas can and lift the hood of his car and start approaching unsuspected individuals with a charming pitch: Hey, how are you doing? I was rushing out of the house and completely forgot to grab my wallet. I was wondering if you could help me out with a little gas money? Taking advantage of his charming demeanor and the allure of his fairly new car usually gets them, makes his story seem pretty real. Mikel, targeted in on single women, who would generously offer financial assistance.

This deceptive tactic not only yielded him monetary gains of two hundred to three hundred daily, within a mere of five hours but also allowed him to collect a decent amount of phone numbers. Despite his illicit success, Mikel's true potential laid dormant, overshadowed by his chosen path of least resistance.

MEET: Amari

Unlike Mikel,

Was not the top student in his class, but he possessed an unyielding ambition and a profound desire to have a better future for himself. Eager to enter the workforce as soon as he was legally able, he encountered initial challenges due to his lack of work experience.

Observing an older teenager from his neighborhood who frequently passed by his house in a McDonald's uniform, Amari decided to seek guidance. Through his thoughtful inquiries, Amari learned that he could apply for a job at McDonald's once he turned 16. With unwavering determination, he pursued this opportunity. Despite facing setbacks and difficulties, Amari, secured a position at the fast food chain. He demonstrated an unparalleled work ethic and commitment, swiftly earning recognition as the most outstanding employee.

Over the course of a decade, he leveraged his dedication and determination to ascend with the company. Eventually, becoming the proud owner of five McDonald's franchises.

Amari's story serves as a testament to the transformative power of hard work and the importance of unleashing one's full potential and persistently striving towards excellence.

In these contrasting narratives, Mikel represents the consequences of underestimating one's abilities and succumbing to the a path of least resistance. While Amari exemplifies the profound impact of determination, hard work, and perseverance and achieving remarkable success.

CHAPTER 8
PROTECT YOUR CROWN

The crown symbolizes you and your LOVE ones, the people you hold dearly to your heart.

The key is to equip oneself with some form of self defense skills, as having no means of protection in today's world can be concerning.

Animals possess natural instincts and physical attributes for survival. For instance, the turtle has it's protective shell, providing a simple yet effective defense mechanism. Similarly, cats rely on their claws and agility for protection. These natural defenses serve as "armor" for these animals in the wild.

In comparison, as humans, we have the capacity to learn and adapt. Allowing us to develop various forms of "armor" for self protection. While formal training in Martial Arts is one option, it's not the only path to personal safety. Cultivating situational awareness, understanding de-escalation techniques, and maintain physical fitness are also valuable ways to enhance self-defense.

It's important to recognize that the goal of self defense is not to seek out confrontation, but rather to promote personal safety and peaceful coexistence. By fostering a combination of awareness and knowledge of basic self-defense principles, individuals can better equip themselves to navigate the world more confidently and responsibly.

The pursuit of Martial Arts, Boxing or Wrestling can certainly be beneficial. However, there are multiple avenues for individuals to develop their own "armor" in today's society.

So there's many ways to protect your crown!!!

Verbal de-escalation technique

Safely walking away

Pepper spray

Stun gun or other small weapons and etc..

It is essential to have full knowledge of how to operate your weapon and understand the laws and regulations pertaining to your protective weapon of choice before usage.

MEET: Cedric

A really cool and down-to- earth kind of guy. Cedric was on his weekly date with his girlfriend, enjoying the night breeze after a nice dinner downtown, when suddenly, three urbanites with a thuggish demeanor appeared, demanding Cedric and his girlfriend to give up their belongings. As he heard the sound of a switchblade, Cedric attempted some de-escalation techniques, creating distance from the individuals while reaching for his wallet. He tossed his wallet on the ground. Cedric could have easily taken on these guys with his decade of training, but he was concerned about his girlfriend. Sometimes, you have to weigh out certain situations.

However, as one of the men bent over to retrieve the wallet, Cedric's girlfriend pulled out some pepper spray from her purse and released it like a skunk under attack- she was so fast!! She sprayed everyone in the circle, including Cedric. Hahaha!!

She grabbed Cedric's wallet and guided him home like a guiding light.

Don and Donna had been neighbors for over two years, living in a quiet and unassuming neighborhood where people mostly kept to themselves. Despite their proximity, they had never really spoken to each other until one fateful day when Donna notice Don in his backyard, earnestly digging up the earth. As she observed him from her own yard, she couldn't help but wonder what he was up to. It seemed like he was trying to start a garden, and Donna, with her fond memories of gardening with her beloved grandmother Betty, felt a surge of excitement at the prospect.

Intrigued and feeling a sense of camaraderie due to her own green thumb, Donna decided to approach Don and offer him some gardening advice. To her surprise, Don was receptive and grateful for her tips. This unexpected interaction led to more frequent conversations between the two, and before long, they found themselves enjoying each other's company and sharing stories about their lives. As they spent more time together, they discovered that they had much in common, and a deep connection began to form between them.

Their newfound friendship eventually blossomed into a romantic relationship, and they found joy in nurturing their bond just as they nurtured their budding garden. They complimented each other perfectly, with Donna's nurturing nature and Don's quiet strength providing a strong foundation for their love.

One sunny afternoon, Don and Donna decided to grab a quick bite to eat at a nearby Wendy's. However, their plans were thwarted by an unexpected long line. Needing to use the restroom, Don excused himself and assured Donna that he would return shortly. Little did he know that he would return to a tense and unsettling situation.

Upon exiting the restroom, Don was alarmed to hear Donna's voice raised in frustration and confrontation. Rushing back to the main area, he found her engaged in a heated argument with a group of unruly individuals who had cut in line in front of her. Without a second thought, Don stepped in to defuse the situation. In a calm and authoritative manner, he addressed the group, emphasizing the need for respect and consideration for others. His words seemed to resonate with one of the men, who intervened to prevent the situation from escalating further. As the tension diffused, the group relented and left the restaurant, leaving Don and Donna to catch their breath and process the intensity of the encounter.

Back in the safety of their neighborhood, Don and Donna reflected on the incident. Donna expressed her admiration for Don's bravery, but also her concern for his well-being. They both acknowledged the importance of standing up for what is right, while also recognizing the need to prioritize personal safety. This shared experience not only brought them closer together but also deepened their mutual respect and understanding.

PROTECT YOUR CROWN!!

CHAPTER 9
DIG DEEPER

In the current era, we find ourselves amidst a vast and interconnected web of information, where numerous avenues exist for retrieving knowledge and insights. However, despite the abundance of resources at our fingertips, there is a tendency among many to accept things at face value, often succumbing to the allure of convenience and ease. The reality is that it only takes a few moments to engage in a quick research endeavor. With the ubiquity of smartphones and access to search engines like Google, anyone can cultivate a spirit of inquiry, actively seeking understanding rather than passively accepting and perpetuating potentially erroneous information. The imperative is clear. Expand your mind, and dig deeper.

In a landscape inundated with misinformation, and where opinions often masquerade as facts, it is crucial to cultivate a healthy skepticism and curiosity. Simply accepting the initial piece of information that comes our way can lead to the perpetuation of inaccuracies and misconceptions. By taking the initiative to delve beneath the surface, we empower ourselves to uncover the truth and gain a more comprehensive understanding of the world around us.

So, let us embrace the spirit of inquiry and critical thinking. Let us challenge ourselves to seek out multiple perspectives, verify the information we encounter, and discern the nuances that shape the narratives we encounter. By doing so, we not only enrich our own knowledge but also contribute to the cultivation of a more informed and discerning society. Therefore, in this age of abundant information, let us make a conscious effort to expand our minds, question assumptions, and above all, dig deeper in our relentless pursuit of truth and understanding.

Moreover, the act of digging deeper extends beyond the realm of information retrieval. It encompasses a broader ethos of curiosity and open-mindedness. It calls upon us to venture beyond the surface, to explore the depths of knowledge, and to grapple with the complexities that underpin our reality.

In a word where sound bites and surface- level understandings often dominate discourse, the ability to dig deeper becomes an invaluable skill. By honing this skill, we equip ourselves with the capacity to navigate the complexities of our interconnected world more adeptly. We become better equipped to discern fact from fiction, to appreciate the nuances of differing perspectives, and to engage in meaningful, informed dialogue with others.

Digging deeper infuses our lives with a sense of purpose and intellectual vigor. It propels us towards self-improvement, and to be open to new ideas.

CHAPTER 10
AWAKEN YOUR VOCABULARY

Allow me to share a couple of tricks that helped me rapidly enhance my vocabulary. It all began with a moment of self reflection during one of my reading sessions. Typically, I would speed through my reading material, quickly grasping the overall message. However, this approach often led me to skip over unfamiliar words. It dawned on me that by doing so, I was depriving myself of the opportunity to expand my vocabulary. I made a conscious decision to change this habit. Instead of glossing over unfamiliar words, I Started jotting them down and delving into their definitions. This simple shift in approach proved to be incredibly effective in broadening my word bank.

In addition to this newfound practice, I began investing in books focused on vocabulary building.

It was during this pursuit that I stumbled upon a truly captivating book on etymology. Exploring the origins of words and understanding their linguistic evolution was a revelation. The knowledge I gained provided a deeper, more profound understanding of the words I encountered. It was as if I had gained mastery over these words; they danced effortlessly in the palms of my hands.

Through these deliberate efforts and newfound resources, my vocabulary underwent a remarkable transformation. I no longer felt limited by unfamiliar words, but rather empowered by them. This journey not only enriched my language skills but also deepened my appreciation for the beauty and intricacy of words.

Anyways, let's take a brief look at the fascinating world of etymology and its practical application.

Consider the Latin word "pede", meaning "foot". From this root, a host of words have sprouted, each with a clear connection to its origin. For instance, "pedestrian, pedal, pedestal, pedicure, quadruped,

Impediment, expedite and expedition" all draw from "pede" and revolve around the concept of the foot. This interconnectedness not only makes these words easier to remember but also illuminates their shared association, enriching our understanding of their meaning. For example, let's use the word "expedite". By dissecting its components through the lens of etymology, we uncover the prefix "ex", signifying "out", and the root "pede", meaning "foot". When we consider this breakdown, "expedite" takes on a vivid imagery: something out of the way of the foot. This interpretation aligns with its modern definition of speeding up a process. The notion of removing obstacles in order to facilitate swift progress becomes palpable. It's as if there is nothing obstructing the path, allowing for unhindered advancement.

In contrast, let's explore the word "impediment", Here, the prefix "im" transforms to "in", indicating "in or into", and we once again encounter the root "pede", denoting "foot". This deconstruction yields a striking revelation: "impediment" signifies something "in the way of the foot", suggesting a barrier or obstruction. This concept is exemplified in the common phase "he has a speech impediment," where something obstructs the individual's ability to speak correctly. The etymological exploration vividly illustrates how the presence or absence of obstacles directly influences the movement and progress of various processes or functions.

I fervently believe that incorporating etymology into our educational programs and systems could significantly enhance everyone's vocabulary. By unveiling the origins and relationships of words, students would not only expand their word bank but also deepen their comprehension and retention of language.

It's essential to recognize that a limited vocabulary can indeed act as a hindrance when attempting to express oneself effectively.

CHAPTER 11
RELATIONSHIPS, FRIENDS OR FOE

Relationships

Navigating relationships in today's world can be a complex endeavor, often resembling the act of skipping a rock across a river – hoping it lands on the other side. Taking the time to truly understand each other's wants and needs is crucial, and rushing into a relationship is rarely beneficial. Its important to go on several dates, gradually getting to know one another and assessing compatibility. It's also essential to acknowledge that no one is perfect, and to carefully weigh the pros and cons of a potential relationship.

While the initial spark of attraction may be intense and exhilaration, maintaining a healthy and fulfilling relationship requires dedicated effort from both parties. This involves being considerate, making the other person feel special and loved, and creating meaningful experiences together. Regular date nights can help foster this connection.

In today's age, the prevalence of social media has undeniably impacted the dating landscape, exposing individuals to potentially unhealthy relationship concepts. It's crucial for individuals to rely on their own understanding, experiences and family principles rather than succumbing to external influences. Patience is key, as bonds need time to develop and grow, much like blossoming flowers.

Remember, taking the time to understand each other, carefully considering the dynamics of a potential relationship, and actively working together to nurture and sustain a loving connection are all vital components of a successful partnership.

Friends

A friendship is a valuable aspect of our lives, with true friends being those who genuinely support us, celebrate our successes, and lend a helping hand when needed. They want us to thrive and succeed in life. On the other hand, there exist individuals who may disguise themselves as friends but harbor harmful intentions. It is vital to understand the nuances of relationships, as time often reveals a person's true character. Hence, maintaining a healthy distance until one truly understands their intentions becomes key. True friends are those who have our best interests at heart . They are sincere in their desire to see us flourish and actively contribute to our growth. They offer encouragement, support and guidance when we face challenges. A friend is someone with whom we can be ourselves, share our dreams and celebrate our victories.

Foes

Foes are individuals who wish us harm or hold malicious intentions. They may disguise themselves as friends, feigning concern or altruism, but their underlying motives are detrimental to our achievements, or spread negativity around us. It is crucial to be vigilant and observe their behavior closely to discern their true intentions.

Keeping a certain level of emotional and physical distance from new acquaintances is a prudent approach. It allows for observation and evaluation of their actions, aligning their words with their deeds. Being cautious does not mean assuming everyone is a foe, but rather exercising discretion, until a clearer picture of their intentions emerges.

Keep in thought, that trust is the foundation of any meaningful relationship. Instead of immediately placing our trust in new individuals, it is wiser to let trust develop organically over time. Gradually sharing personal information, experiences and vulnerabilities can help assess if the other person is trustworthy. Trust should be earned through consistent actions rather than granted blindly.

MEET: Mike

A sociable extrovert, who enjoys unwinding on the weekends, by socializing and meeting new people. One weekend, he struck up a conversation with a captivating young woman at his favorite bar, where they bonded over their shared love for wings and many things. Their connection was instant, and they decided to continue the evening at Mike's place, they enjoyed each other's company and shared many laughs.

Despite their deepening connection, Mike never anticipated any malicious intent from the young woman, feeling entirely at ease in her presence. As the night unfolded, they engaged in heartfelt conversation, with Mike even sharing details about his daily routines and schedule.

A week later, while Mike was diligently at work, his newfound companion unexpectedly made her way to his house. Upon Mike's return home, he found his house completely empty and never heard a sound from the beautiful woman again. Mike was left to wonder about the true nature of the woman he had welcomed into his life.

Conclusion:

Distinguishing between friends and foes can be challenging, but through careful observation and maintaining a healthy distance, one can gain clarity on a person's true character and intentions. Patience and discernment are essential nurturing genuine friendships while protecting ourselves from potential harm. Remember, true friends uplift and empower us, making our lives more joyful and fulfilling.

CHAPTER 12
FINANCES/INVESTING/CREDIT/ RETIREMENT

Financial institutions, like banks, indeed have various procedures and products that may not always be transparent to the general public. One such example is the existence of high-interest savings accounts that offer better returns compared to regular savings accounts. It's important to understand that banks are profit-oriented businesses, and their primary objective is to generate revenue.

To attract a larger customer base, banks often promote regular savings accounts that offer relatively low interest rates. These accounts allow the bank to pool funds from numerous customers and lend that money to borrowers at higher interest rates, thereby generating profits. However, the availability of better savings options may not be widely advertised, as it could potentially impact the bank's quarterly bonuses, which are often based on the number of new regular savings accounts opened.

That being said, if you are starting to save money, a regular savings account can still be a suitable option in the initial stages. It provides a secure place to accumulate your funds. However, once you have accumulated a substantial amount, it is advisable to explore other financial instruments that offer higher interest rates.

Here are a few examples of such instruments:

1. Certificate of Deposit (CDs): CDs are time deposits with fixed maturity dates and typically offer higher interest rates compared to regular savings accounts. They require you to deposit a specific amount of money for a predetermined period, and in return, you receive interest upon maturity.

2. Jumbo CDs: Jumbo CDs are similar to regular CDs but require a larger minimum deposit. In exchange for the larger deposit, you can often earn higher interest rates.

3. Money Market Accounts: Money Market Accounts are interest-bearing accounts that usually have higher interest rates than regular savings accounts. They often require a higher minimum balance, but they may provide additional benefits such as check- writing privileges.

It's important to carefully review the terms, conditions, and interest rates associated with these financial instruments before making a decision. Additional, consider consulting with a financial advisor or representative from the financial institution to ensure you select the most suitable option based on your specific goals and circumstances.

Now that you saved, you can upgrade your investing status. You put in the hard work!!! As a featherweight, you learned to bomb and weave the norm. You saved and invested on a smaller scale but it is time to level up and build your financial nest with diversity and uniqueness. It's time to follow the guiding light.

Below, I've put together some more financial instrument to consider:

1. Dividend Stocks: These stocks are typically issued by well established, stable companies known as blue-chip companies. They pay out a portion of their profits to shareholders in the form of dividends, often on a quarterly basis. Investors can benefit from regular income in addition to potential capital appreciation.

2. Index Funds: An index fund is a type of mutual fund or exchange-traded fund (ETF) that aims to replicate the performance of a specific market index, such as the S&P 500. By

investing in a diverse range of stocks within the index, investors can potentially achieve returns that mirror the overall market performance, often averaging around 10% annually.

3. Bonds: Bonds are debt securities issued by governments, municipalities, or corporations to raise capital. When an investor buys a bond, they are essentially lending money to the issuer in exchange for periodic interest payments and the return of the bond's face value at maturity. Bonds are generally considered less risky than stocks and can provide a steady stream of income.

4. Binary Options: Binary Options are a type of financial derivative that offers a fixed payout if the underlying asset meets predetermined conditions within a specified time frame. Investors either receive a predetermined amount of cash or nothing at all, depending on whether their prediction about the price

movement of the underlying asset is correct. In all honesty, I love Binary Options!!!

5. Bitcoin: Bitcoin is a digital or virtual currency that operates on a decentralized network known as blockchain. Investors can buy bitcoin through cryptocurrency exchanges or online platforms and store it in digital wallets. The price of bitcoin can fluctuate significantly over short periods, and investors often buy and hold the cryptocurrency as a long-term investment, speculating that its value will increase over time.

Ultimately, investing in these financial instruments requires a thorough understanding of the investment and a willingness to accept the associated risks, including the potential for both significant gains and losses.

Closing this chapter without mentioning my favorite investment instrument would have been a sin.

REAL ESTATE

Real estate investing has evolved significantly over time. While traditional methods of securing bank loans for property purchases remain prevalent, new avenues have emerged. Many investors now engage private and hard money lenders to finance various real estate ventures, such as personal residence acquisitions, house flipping, wholesaling, and rental properties.

Moreover, creative strategies, including owner financing, assuming mortgages, assuming taxes, and navigating foreclosure properties, have gained traction among real estate investors. These innovative approaches offer opportunities to acquire properties with unique financial structures.

Real estate stands out as a favored investment avenue due to its potential for long-term appreciation, passive income generation through rentals, and the various strategies available for profit generation. Many investors view real estate as a cornerstone of their investment portfolios due to its historically proven ability to generate wealth and hedge against inflation.

In conclusion, real estate offers unique advantages in the investment ring, and its dynamic nature continues to attract investors to go after that financial champion belt that real estate provides. My question to you, "are you ready for your champion belt?"

CREDIT

It's crucial to understand the immense importance of your credit score, as it holds a similar level of significance to other personal numbers such as your social security number, ID number, phone number, or even the number of your significant other. Your credit score can have a profound impact on your financial life, yet many people tend to overlook its importance.

To illustrate the significance of having good credit, let's consider the scenarios of two individuals named Alanda & Eurius. Both Alanda and Eurius are hardworking and motivated individuals who have decided to buy a house to start their new families. However, their credit scores differ significantly. Unfortunately, Alanda's credit score is not very good, resulting in the bank offering him a loan with a ridiculously high interest rate.

For instance, let's say the house that Alanda is looking to purchase costs $150,000 with added interest, the total cost of the house becomes $220,000. On the other hand, Eurius has an excellent credit score, which enables him to secure a loan with a much more favorable interest rate. Considering that Eurius is purchasing the same exact house for $ 150,000, with the interest added, the total cost for him comes to $ 175,000.

The difference in having good credit versus bad credit becomes apparent here. Eurius, with his good credit score, is able to save a significant amount of money, amounting to $45,000, compared to Alanda. This demonstrates how having good credit can have a tremendous positive impact on your financial situation.

A good credit score not only affects your ability to obtain favorable loan terms when buying a house but also affects other areas of your financial life. It can determine the interest rates you receive on car loans, affect your chances of being approved for an apartment rental, and can even impact your employability in certain fields.

Building and maintaining good credit is achievable through consistent and responsible financial habits. This includes paying bills on time, managing credit accounts responsibly, and keeping your credit utilization low. Regularly monitoring and reviewing your credit report for any inaccuracies and taking steps to correct them are also crucial.

I personally used these apps to build my credit:

1. Kikoff
2. Self
3. Grow Credit
4. Credit Karma
5. Credit Sesame

Definitely check them out and see if they fit your credit building needs.

Retirement

It's important to have a retirement plan in place, and implementing one of the below instruments is crucial for a comfortable retirement.

A 401(k) plan is a retirement savings account offered by many employers. It allows employees to contribute a portion of their pre-tax salary to a retirement account, where the money can grow tax- deferred until retirement. Some employers also match a portion of an employee's contributions, which can significantly boost retirement savings. When you retire, you can begin withdrawing from your 401(k) account, and these withdrawals are taxed as regular income.

Individual Retirement Accounts (IRAs)

IRAs are personal retirement savings accounts that offer tax advantages to individuals. There are two main types of IRAs: traditional and Roth. With a traditional IRA, Contributions may be tax-deductible, and the money grows tax-deferred until withdrawal, at which point it is taxed as regular income. With a Roth IRA, contributions are made with after tax dollars, but qualified withdrawals in retirement are tax free. IRAs are not tied to employment, so individuals can open and contribute to an IRA on their own.

Social Security:

Social Security is a federal benefits program that provides financial support to retirees, as well as to the disabled, survivors, and their families. Workers contribute to Social Security through payroll taxes, and those who qualify are eligible to receive benefits in retirement.

The failure to set up a solid but reliable plan for retirement can result in one re-entering the workforce, there's many factors to consider while planning for retirement. Inflation seems to be a big factor in most of these cases.

Creating a realistic budget and understanding ones desired lifestyle in retirement are crucial aspects of a solid retirement plan. By carefully planning for ongoing expenses and considering the potential impact of inflation on the cost of living, retirees can better prepare for the long-term financial demands of retirement without the need to re-enter the workforce.

Meet: Ryan

Ryan retired at the age of 65, faced with many financial difficulties. Unfortunately, had to re-enter the workforce 5 years later after enjoying a more relaxed pace of life. Ryan is trying to adapt to his new routines and high demands at work, dealing with workplace dynamics and managing job related stress can be emotionally taxing, especially after being away from the workforce for an extended period.

A month or two later, Ryan had a heart attack at the work place and was hospitalized for a few weeks.

I cannot stress it enough, please seek guidance from financial advisors, retirement planners, and other professionals can be invaluable in constructing a retirement plan that is solid in the face of inflation.

By developing and implementing a comprehensive retirement plan, seniors can strive to enjoy their well-deserved retirement years with confidence, financial security, and peace of mind. This approach can help ensure that their retirement remains a time for relaxation, pursuing personal interests, and cherishing moments with loved ones, without the emotional and financial strains that may arise from the need to re-entering the workforce like Ryan.

CHAPTER 13
LIFE INSURANCE, WILL, AND FUNERAL RELATED MATTERS.

Life insurance plays a crucial role in providing financial security for your loved ones, especially in the event of your untimely death. By having life insurance in place, you can ensure that your family members are not left with a financial burden. They can use the proceeds from the policy to cover living expenses, pay off debts, and plan without worrying about financial instability.

There are several types of life insurance, including term life, whole life, and universal life insurance. Each type has its own features, benefits, and costs. Here's a brief overview of each:

1. Term Life Insurance: Provides coverage for a specific period (10, 20, or 30 years). It is straightforward and generally more affordable, offering a death benefit if you die within the term.

2. Whole Life Insurance: Offers coverage for your entire life and includes a cash value component that grows over time. It is more expensive but provides lifelong protection and an investment component.

3. Universal Life Insurance: offers flexibility in premium payments and death benefits. It also includes a cash value component and allows for adjustments in coverage and premiums.

There are many Life Insurance companies to choose from, but always be inquisitive about the terms and regulations before purchasing a policy.

HAVING A WILL

MEET: Malikai, Unfortunately, he passed away at the age of 78 without putting a will in place. Malikai was a successful entrepreneur who owned a small printing company and had amassed a substantial collection of assets, including multiple houses, antique cars, motorcycles, and various investments. Despite his achievements, the absence of a clear and adamant will has led to turmoil within his once –loving family. The lack of a will has resulted in bitter disputes over Malikai's possessions, tearing the family apart.

Malikai's story underscores the critical importance of having a will in place. A will is a legal document that outlines a person's wishes regarding the distribution of their assets and the care of any dependents after their death. Without a will, the distribution of assets and the resolution of potential disputes can become complex and contentious, as seen in Malikai's case. To obtain a good will, one should consult with an experienced attorney who specializes in estate planning and wills. They can guide you through the process and help you draft a will that accurately reflects your wishes.

In conclusion, Malikai's story serves as a poignant reminder of the importance of setting a will in place to protect one's legacy and to provide a peace of mind for loved ones.

Funeral related matters

I understand that funerals can be incredibly difficult for all of us. The passing of someone we hold dearly in our hearts can be truly devastating.

Losing my parents was an experience that reshaped my world in ways I never imagined. They were not just my parents; they were my best friends, confidants, and my unwavering sources of love and guidance. Their passing left a void that seemed impossible to fill. As I grappled with the overwhelming waves of grief, I found peace in the memories we shared and the profound impact they had on my life. Reflecting on the experiences and wisdom my parents imparted, I realized that their legacy extended far beyond their physical presence. Their enduring love and the lessons they taught me became my guiding light. Unfortunately, losing love ones is inevitable and difficult.

Below are some factors to consider when losing someone you love:

1.   Dealing with the funeral home:

When a loved one passes away, the family typically contacts a funeral home to make arrangements. The funeral home director will guide the family through the process and make necessary arrangements for transporting the deceased to the funeral home.

Planning the funeral:

The funeral director will help the family plan the funeral or memorial service. This includes deciding on date, time, and location of the service, as well as selecting a casket, arranging for flowers, and preparing an obituary.

Legal and administrative aspect:

The funeral home will assist the family in obtaining the necessary legal documents, such as the death certificate, and may help with notifying Social Security, the veteran's administration, and other relevant organizations.

2.   Purchasing a plot and stone:

If the deceased is to be buried, the family will need to select a cemetery and purchase a burial plot. The funeral home can often assist in making these arrangements or provide recommendations.

Choosing a headstone or grave marker:

The family may also choose a headstone or grave marker to mark the grave. This involves selecting the type of stone, design, and inscription. The funeral home or cemetery can provide guidance on this process.

3.   Option for burial:

Traditional burial: In a traditional burial, the deceased is place in a casket and interred in the ground at a cemetery. This typically involves a graveside service.

Cremation: Cremation is an increasingly popular option. In this process, the body is reduced to ashes through intense heat. The family can then decide to keep the ashes in an urn, scatter them in a meaningful location, share them amongst family members, or bury them in a cemetery.

4. Enhancements and considerations:

Families often choose to personalize the funeral or service with special music, readings, or displays that reflect the life and interests of the deceased.

Pre-planning: Some individuals choose to pre-plan their funerals to alleviate the burden on their loved ones. This allows the person to make their own arrangements for their funeral, burial, or cremation and specify their preferences.

Overall, the funeral process involves working closely with the funeral home to make arrangements for the service, selecting a burial plot and stone if necessary, and making decisions about the method of disposition, whether through traditional burial or cremation. Each step involves careful consideration and personalization to honor the life of your passed loved one.

First, I want to express my heartfelt gratitude to you for journeying through the pages of "Guiding Light."

Your attention and engagement with this book have truly meant the world to me. It is my sincerest hope that the chapters within these pages have served as beacons of enlightenment, inspiration, and knowledge, expanding your understanding and enriching your perspective in profound ways.

Throughout "Guiding Light," I've endeavored to shine a light on the often overlooked aspects of life, emphasizing how these seemingly small elements can serve as fundamental building blocks that fortify our very foundation. Every chapter has been carefully crafted, and interwoven with explicit examples, all with the intention of empowering and uplifting you.

As you reach the conclusion of this book, my fervent wish is that "Guiding Light" continues to accompany you on your journey of self-improvement. May the wisdom and insights contained within these pages resonate with you, guiding you as you navigate the complexities of life and encouraging you to strive for personal growth and fulfillment.

Now, the time has come for you to embrace the best version of yourself. Let the light within you shine brightly, illuminating your way forward and inspiring others around you.

In closing, I extend my warmest wishes for your future endeavors. May you continue to seek knowledge, cultivate positivity, and embrace the endless possibilities that lie ahead. Thank you once again for allowing "Guiding Light" to be a part of your life's journey.

With heartfelt gratitude and warm regards,

Mike Hall

POEM

Confidence now at soaring heights,

I spread my wings,

Embrace the sights.

No hesitation, no fear in sight,

Ill dominate and earn ovation's rights.

Learned to navigate through life's formations,

Setting goals, discerning friends from falsifications.

Standing firm, even when the world imposes,

Thanks to the Guiding Light, that forever imposes.

With each word read, my spirit arose.

A beacon of hope, my Guiding Light bestows

Printed in the USA
CPSIA information can be obtained
at www.ICGtesting.com
CBHW040341240324
5746CB00009B/88